SEE THROUGH

WORDS TO FEEL OR FEELINGS IN WORDS

ANJALI SINGH CHANDEL

Copyright © Anjali Singh Chandel
All Rights Reserved.

ISBN 979-888606512-1

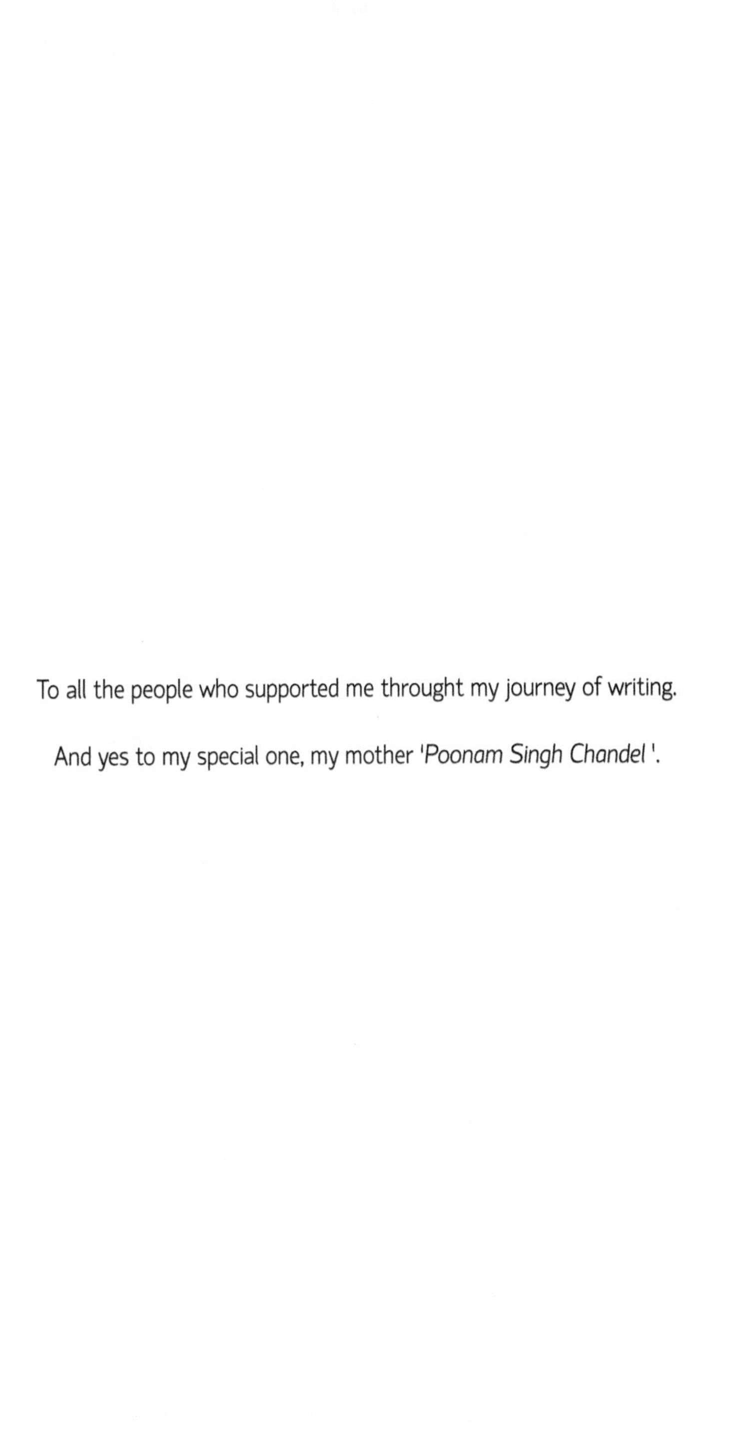

To all the people who supported me throught my journey of writing.

And yes to my special one, my mother 'Poonam Singh Chandel '.

Contents

Contents

See Through

Feelings or words to feel.

Even my pen changes colour

while writing down stories.

But in your case, the story repesents a single colour,

the colour of different vibes, the beautiful ones.

Scattered parts of me lies beautifully to the world,

but in front of you it speaks gloriously.

I want to carry the smile with you which my mother
carried before.

Rain and songs bring memories back,

memories you encounter daily.

The street is quiet,

and the heart is loud.

Mind is wondering and so do legs are trembling.

Weird how night plays it game.

Moon even has it's different phases and finally

comes full.

I wanna break all my emotions and feel

nothing less than being free.

Sleepy eyes, not searching anymore.

Wind breezing, mind Wondering.

Melodies of old cassettes.

Cup of hot tea in summers.

Decorating new wardrobe of thoughts.

Feeling yourselves, accepting.

Dancing bare foot to feel that rhythm.

Today, I wake up early in order to hide from flashbacks.

Reading quotes, I'm getting your vibes again.

How come I don't think of anything else other than you?

I always ask this question from myself.

Maybe I loved you too fiercely burning my own wings.

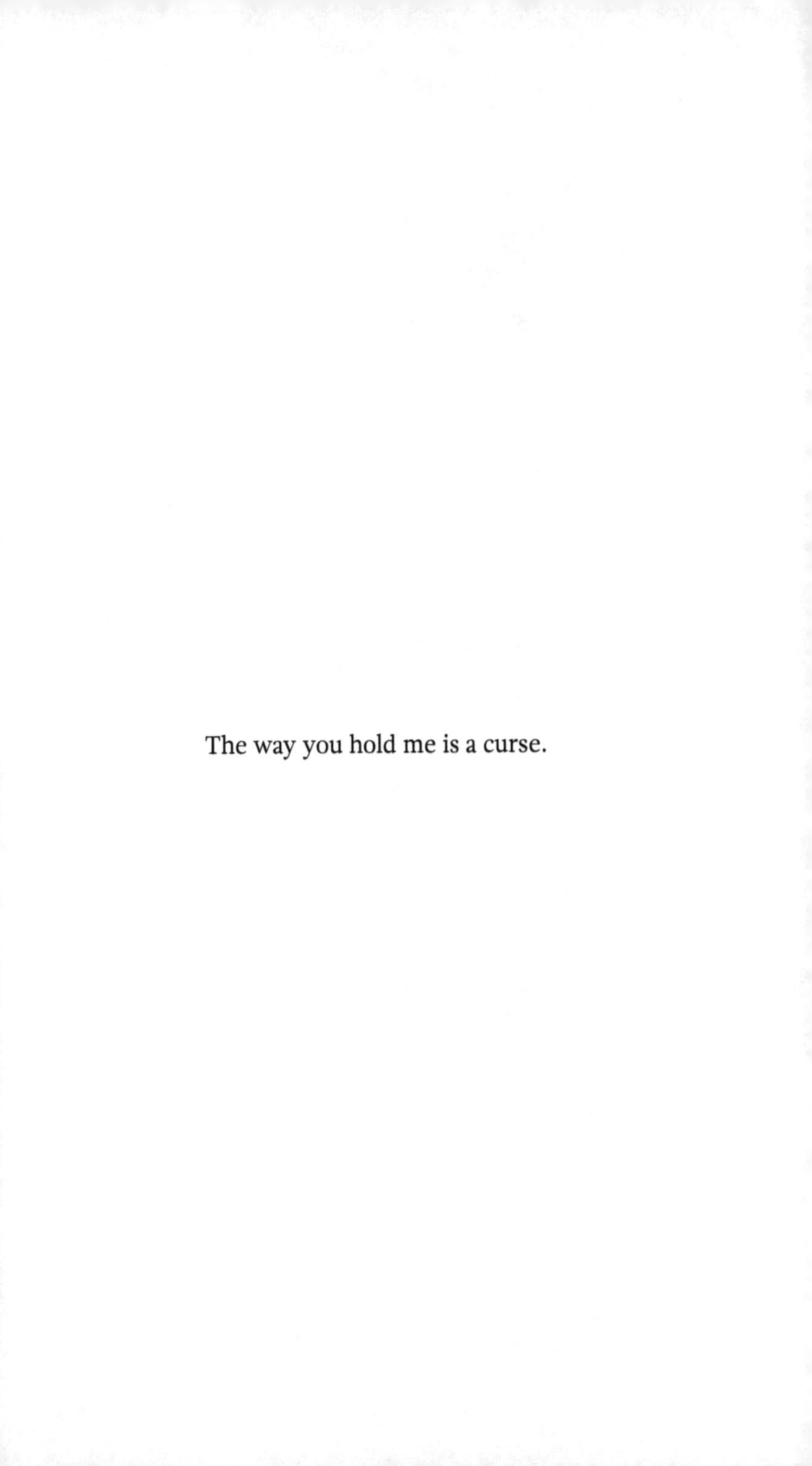

The way you hold me is a curse.

Somewhere heard that feeling too

Brutally can mentally destroy you.

If so then make it a deal with flowers for my mourning,

when I'll pass leaving sparkles of happy memories,

as my sparkles are left behind dust for you which will
vanish.

Maybe I'm shattered like stars in the dark sky.

But the sparkling is just a illusion of happiness.

The sheet is covered with wishes of neighbourhood.

Even if you are not with me,

I feel some part of you is always around me.

I see you smile from distance between our eyes.

And will love you from distance between our eyes.

To turn me into an open book,

the world has to be recreated again with the

hope of ' loving each scars'.

Even the greatest night encounters sorrow and happiness
together.

Binding illusion to this world of craft,

Sculpturing the inner soul to be covered by outer story.

Hindering in the forest of memories.

Hiking on the mountains alone.

Swimming on the deepest possible ocean of thoughts.

Carving you in parts,

I want to make you whole.

The breeze is soothing,

touching the hairs with sounds of unsaid words,

silence is all around but

the heart is popping around.

Holding your hands,

walking desperately to low the noise of a beautiful sound.

Chaos in mind.

Still heart is pumping,

confused and calm at the same point.

I want it bad, there is but.

There is truth hidden I wanna explore.

Wondering if everything said is unsaid why ?

I can't get my mind alarm silent for a second.

I'm too fierce to see the unsaid, undone, done and said
clearly.

I want distance to be filled with happy child like
innocence.

I want constant mind junction to become a single lane.

I want a long never ending journey of craft I baked.

Just hearing voices.

I touched my skin today and it felt smooth.

Maybe that roughness is healing,

I can feel myself again.

A happy soul,

a real laughter,

a real smile.

What else I can dress up with ?

Sitting under the sky,

hearing noises.

That beauty of different sounds,

exterior and interior along.

That memories blending with the peace today.

I felt sudden urge to be heard by me.

Each scar love it's mark,

Each mark love it's existence.

Every time I feel this constant rush going through my
mind.

I feel dizzy.

Don't know where all this going to end.

Crumpled visuals, that's all I have.

I want to fly high and I guess I'm on my way.

The sheet is covered with stains of illusion.

See through yet false.

Flesh is new and raw.

Not moulding itself, just free.

Words often lie,

Maybe to protect their weakness,

or to endure happiness.

My pen creates illusion just like the moon,

make you feel the reality of hidden soul.

These vague figures are carrying life,

hilariously immortal ones.

I sit in dark room in order to hide my scream,

the pain I suffer daily.

The more I'm likely to be free, the more I'm in pain.

Suddenly the light strikes my darkness,

happiness knocked my door.

And again I suffer more darkness living in the light itself.

Profundity of words may be false,

But that feeling never lies.

Whatever happening inside is more than a thunderstorm.

Carrying bleeding draft, pouring on you.

Making you stone.

Even now nostalgia hits me harder.

Even now I have glimpse of you.

Even now words roam in my head.

Even now I can hear that whispering of yours.

Even now.

Yes I'm weird,

Yes I laugh all the time,

Yes I have the brightest smile.

(Yes I'm the pain,

Yes I'm the strongest game)

Yes that's me four letter word 'love'.

If you can't handle my weirdness, how will

you than handle the promises of future?

What are prayers actually?

The one with lust or the one with true love.

Curtains are covering the eyes of people

and always will but who cares

when my people is you.

Knock Knock the feelings are about to burst.

Just waiting to explore the darkness with red flame.

Of whatever butterflies it may turned out to be.

Shine is dim and bright at the same time.

Playing it's game like never before.

Mastering it's sculpture to be the part of hidden soul.

Author

The journey has just started with this first book of her ' SEE THROUGH '.There is a lot to go and she finds it fascinating, words and she the perfect combo.

www.ingramcontent.com/pod-product-compliance
Lightning Source LLC
Chambersburg PA
CBHW021136130726
47988CB00003B/1334